NORWICH
Volume 4

A Fourth Portrait in Old Picture Postcards

by

Philip Standley

S. B. Publications

By the same author: Norwich, Volumes 1, 2 and 3

First published in 1992 by S. B. Publications
c/o 19 Grove Road, Seaford, East Sussex, BN25 1TP.

ISBN 1 85770 032 5

Typeset and printed by Geo. R. Reeve Ltd., Wymondham, Norfolk NR18 0BD.

CONTENTS

CONTENTS

CONTENTS

Cover Picture: St. Stephen's Street, c. 1904.

INTRODUCTION

When I was first asked to write Volume 1, I never thought that I would be writing Volume 4! Little did I realise the interest the first book would receive nor how the series would develop with two further volumes, all of which have since been reprinted. My publisher and I have had repeated enquiries about a forth volume so, with the help and generosity of friends who have excellent collections of old postcards — Rhoda Bunn, Michael Dixon, Basil Gowen, Eric Read and Tony Williamson — along with a further selection from my own collection, I have assembled this new book — Norwich Volume 4, in which I trust you will find many hours of nostalgic memories.

Once again, we have tried to make this a tour of Norwich and its outskirts. The illustrations form a route from the Market Place to Haymarket, Bethel Street, St. Giles, College Road, St. Stephen's Road, Queen's Road, St. Stephen's Street, Orford Place, Prince of Wales Road, Thorpe Road, St. Benedict's Street, Magdalen Street, Aylsham Road and, completing the collection, a selection of disasters, events, village scenes and advertisements. Where possible, I have cross-referenced this book with the other three volumes.

I am grateful for all the help and advice given to me by many friends, and to my wife, Mary, and daugther, Sarah, for sorting out my notes and typing. Also, may I take this oppotunity of thanking you, the readers, for your many appreciative letters and for adding further information to the postcard captions which were difficult to research. I would still like to see any unusual postcards of Norwich — who knows, there may even be a Volume 5!

Philip Standley,
Wymondham,
October, 1992.

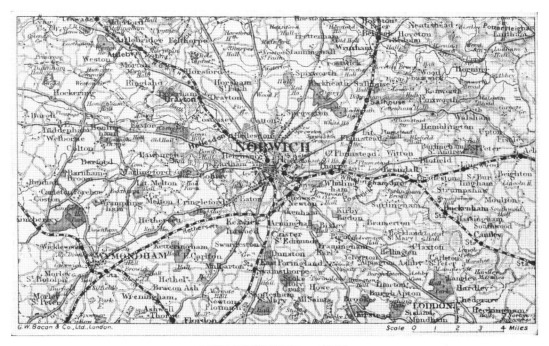

MAP POSTCARD, c. 1906

Published by G. W. Bacon Co. Ltd,. of London, these postcards covered the whole country and featured a specific area within a county or the county itself. This card shows Norwich and its surrounding towns and villages. It is particularly interesting because it shows Norwich's three railway termini — City, Thorpe and Victoria — along with the railway routes served by the Great Eastern Railway and the Midland and Great Northern Joint Railway. In addition, the map shows the road network before the building of the Ring Road and the inner relief road.

MARKET PLACE, c. 1930

An unusual wide-angle view of the Market Place, this would have been taken when the stalls were cleared away at weekends. On the left is St. Peter Mancroft Church; next is the tin hut used by the police from 1911 to April 1938 as the force headquarters, and then the Municipal Buildings. At the rear of these buildings, to the right, can be seen the demolition work being carried out for the construction of the City Hall. Notice the tram lines on Guildhall Hill and the policeman in white coat and helmet — with no traffic to direct!

MARKET PLACE AND GUILDHALL, c. 1930

These views provide an interesting comparison with traffic conditions today. The Walk is now pedestrianised and, in front of the Guildhall, there is a taxi rank. The postcard on the right shows the Raven public house, located in the centre background between the City Hall and the Guildhall, which was badly damaged in the 1942 blitz.
(M. Dixon collection)

CHURCH BELLS OF ST. PETER MANCROFT, c. 1925

According to a plaque in the Ringing Chamber, these bells were rehung in memory of Alexander Chamberlin, by his daughter, Agnes Mary Clarke, on 19th April, 1925. This postcard shows the bells in the process of being rehung. The first recorded true peal of bells at St. Peter Mancroft was rung in 1715, by the 'Norwich Scholars' as the ringers were then known. The largest bell, the tenor, weighs about two tons.

(A. Williamson collection)

4

THE HAYMARKET

In the left background, the shops in view include Green's, outfitters, and the International Stores. The Haymarket Cinema, on the right, was showing 'Change of Heart' starring Janet Gaynor and Charles Farrell. In the centre background is Orford Place and in the foreground is the statue of Sir Thomas Browne.
(R. Bunn collection)

HAYMARKET, NORWICH. (321.)   G.1661.

TANK WEEK, c. 1917

Tank Week was held in all the major towns and cities of the country to raise money for the war effort by promoting the sale of war bonds. This postcard shows the arrival of the tank and its progress along the Walk — passing Green's — accompanied by troops and police. (For further details see Volume 1, page 110).

(A. Williamson collection)

FATHER CHRISTMAS IN LONDON STREET, c. 1923

Father Christmas arrives at Jarrold's Store in London Street — an annual event which continues today. He is seen here sitting on top of a coach with hundreds of children and adults in attendance. The tram in the background — going up Guildhall Hill — also appears to be surrounded by a crowd.

(A. Williamson collection)

CHAMBERLIN'S SHOWROOM, c. 1912

The interior of this drapery showroom shows the different approach to business in those days with chairs for the customers and the counters and shelves behind well-stocked with goods. The exterior of the shop is shown in Volume 1, on page 2. Chamberlin's is now a Tesco Store.

(B. Gowen collection)

THE FISH MARKET

The old fish market was situated on the east side of St. Peter's Street. This moved to Mountergate in 1913. In the background, the church of St. Peter Mancroft is shown before the addition of its four octagonal turrets. The artist of the above picture was D. Hodgson.

BETHEL STREET, c. 1931

On the extreme left is the yard of Lacy and Lincoln and, next door, is the Coachmakers Arms. The 'Coachmakers' and the rest of the left-hand buildings were demolished in 1934 to make way for the new Fire Station. The tower of St. Peter Mancroft Church can be seen in the right background with the Bethel Hospital on the right.
(E. J. Read collection)

BETHEL STREET, c. 1912

Looking towards St. Giles, the buildings on the left still stand. The three-storey building, in the centre, also remains — minus its sign board — and the confectionery shop of G. Bacon, to the left of the archway, is now an office. In the right foreground, numbers 42 and 44 were the headquarters of the 2nd East Anglian Field Ambulance (R.A.M.C.) Territorial Force. In 1912, the commanding officer was Colonel J. M. G. Bremner, O.B.E. Today, this elaborate Edwardian building, built at the turn of the century, is occupied by the Modern Press.
(A. Williamson collection)

MR. RAYMOND, 1a St. Giles Gates, NORWICH. *Artificial Teeth.*

Series by the Scottish Photographic Touring and Pictorial Post Card Co ., Glasg;w.

MR RAYMOND, 1a ST. GILES GATES, c. 1905

Mr Raymond made artificial teeth and was photographed attending to a customer in a very robust and non-reclining chair, in what looks like an ordinary Victorian sitting room. Notice the oil lamp and the aspidistra on the table. Mr Raymond probably commissioned the postcard to advertise his services; this one was posted on 30th June, 1905.
(R. Bunn collection)

THE NORWICH CITADEL CONCERTINA BAND, c. 1908

Twenty-five members of the Concertina Band — plus one violinist and one drummer — were photographed in an unknown location. Could it be in the grounds of the Citadel in St. Giles Street? One clue is the statue of a stag in the left background. Today, the Salvation Army is usually associated with silver or brass bands.

THE SPEAR IN HAND, VAUXHALL STREET

This is a very rare photograph showing the interior of the Spear in Hand public house, 27 Vauxhall Street, owned by Bullard's Brewery. Rum, brandy, whisky and gin barrels are on display plus many bottles. Notice the advertisement for England's Glory Matches and the picture of the King on the wall. Can any reader identify the landlord?

(E. J. Read collection)

THE SOLDIERS' MEMORIAL, NORWICH CEMETERY

In 1875, several acres of land were added to Norwich Cemetery and the first grave to be dug there was for a soldier. This led to a section being set aside for soldiers who died whilst stationed at Norwich and it was decided that a suitable monument should be erected. Funds were raised and, in due course, the memorial was built; it is 21ft. high with the statue being 7ft. high. The memorial was unveiled by Lord Waveney in October, 1978.

41, NEWMARKET STREET, c. 1915

Mr Edward Smith, printer, bookbinder, newsagent and tobacconist, stands outside his shop located at the junction of Newmarket and York Streets. Advertising posters and signs include: on the walls — Reeve's Marvel rubber heels; St. Julien Tobacco and Capstan cigarettes; on the shop front — Will's Gold Flake, priced at 10 for 3d. and Stephens Ink. The fly sheets include *The People, The Sunday Pictorial, The Dispatch, The Sunday Herald* and *The News of the World* — presumably the photograph was taken on a Sunday. The headlines referring to a coal strike, war work for women and pictures of the trenches indicate that it was the summer of 1915. Today, the corner shop is a Happy Shopper general store.

(R. Bunn collection)

ONLEY STREET, c. 1912

Onley Street runs from Unthank Road to Leicester Street. In the left foreground, the sun blinds belong to Minn's Bakery, now occupied by Sewell's Bakery. In the distance is the junction with Durham Street. On the extreme right, at No. 1, Onley Street, the grocery shop belonged to Mr Horatio George Empson and has the usual advertisements which include Cadbury's cocoa, Oxo cubes and Camp coffee. Today, this shop is Grove Stores. The houses are much the same now — a typical Norwich street.

17

GLOUCESTER STREET, c. 1912

E. C. Jeary, ladies' and gentlemen's tailors, stood at the junction of Unthank Road and Gloucester Street. The building is much the same today but the creeper has disappeared from the wall and, with today's traffic, it is not such a tranquil scene.The Clean Machine launderette now occupies these premises. The post office on the opposite corner of this junction is shown in Volume 1, on page 20.

(A. Williamson collection)

NORWICH TRAINING COLLEGE FROM COLLEGE ROAD. 4 7854 (*Jarrolds' Series*)

NORWICH TRAINING COLLEGE, COLLEGE ROAD, c. 1910

The Norwich Diocesan Training College was founded in 1839, in the Cathedral Close. In 1853, it moved to St. George's Plain where it remained until 1892 when the buildings on College Road were opened. These buildings were designed by Oliver & Leeson of Newcastle upon Tyne, with building costs totalling £14,000. The college was destroyed by fire during the blitz of 1942.

THE NETBALL TEAM, 1918-19

The Norwich Diocesan Training College Junior Netball team were photographed in the grounds of the college. From left to right , the ladies are: *(back row)* Edna Burgess, Hilda Boddy and Annie Dickinson; *(front row)* Evelyn Goman, Nellie Howard (Captain), Miss Roscoe, Dorothy Thompson and Alice Oakes.

AVENUE ROAD SCHOOL

The School stands on the corner of Swansea and Milford Roads and is still in use today. It has lost its spire and many of the decorative corners, but the sign in the brickwork — "Board School, Boys and Girls" — remains. In 1912, it had accommodation for 775 children and 314 infants. Kelly's Directory for 1922 records that there were 368 boys under the control of Mr F. T. Oxbury, headmaster, 366 girls under Miss D. Shreeve, headmistress, and 248 infants with Miss L. A. Olley in charge.

BRUNSWICK ROAD, 1912

Looking down Brunswick Road from Newmarket Road, the wall and railings on the left are still there today. The first junction on the left is Hanover Road, then there is Trix Road and, further along, Newmarket Street, Cambridge Street and Trinity Street. The houses on the right were demolished to make way for the new Norfolk & Norwich Hospital and car park. Union Street can just be seen in the right background.

(E. J. Read collection)

NEWMARKET ROAD, c. 1910

The number 37 tram from Thorpe Road is seen heading towards Newmarket Road at the junction of Ipswich and Grove Roads. The railings of the Norfolk & Norwich Hospital can be seen on the left. Many of the trees have now disappeared.

ST. STEPHEN'S ROAD, p.u. 1908

Photographed at the junction of St. Stephen's and Kingsley Roads, the notice on the three-storey house states: "These buildings will be remodelled and refronted. See particulars of sale". Was the end of this house pulled down to make way for Kingsley Road? To the left of the picture is Victoria Street. Notice the tram standard and the young boy who stands for the photographer under the gas lamp.

(A. Williamson collection)

CITY WALLS, COBURG STREET

Coburg Street ran from St. Stephen's to Chapelfield East. Now only a small part of Coburg Street remains at the Chapelfield end of Malthouse Lane, the remainder being part of the Nestle Mackintosh factory. The buildings being demolished here backed on to the City Walls in Coburg Street — the same as those in Chapelfield Road which were later demolished to make way for the dual carriageway. The walls were then preserved and are still there today.
(B. Gowen collection)

QUEEN'S ROAD

Another photograph by Tom Nokes, the Norwich photographer, this was taken outside the Lame Dog public house on the corner of Queen's Road and All Saints Green. It shows members of the Ladies Social Club and is dated 9th July, 1924. The clothes worn by the ladies are most interesting, particularly the hats — notice the back row — but what was the occasion? Another view of the public house is shown in Volume 1, on page 6.

(R. Bunn collection)

PRIMITIVE METHODIST CHAPEL, QUEEN'S ROAD

This chapel stands on the west side of Queen's Road. It was designed by the Norwich architect, Edward Boardman, and built in 1872. It closed for worship in the early 1950s and has since been converted into offices and named St. Francis House. The railings have disappeared but otherwise the building remains the same today.

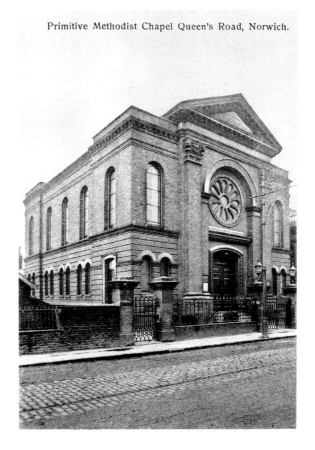

Primitive Methodist Chapel Queen's Road, Norwich.

HOME & COLONIAL STORES, c. 1916

The manager and three of his staff standing outside the Home and Colonial Stores at 18 St. Stephen's Street, were photographed on a damp and dismal day. The right-hand window displays an advertisement for 'Perfect' margarine and, on the far right, the display board reads: 'Robertson's mineral water manufacturers, caterer and confectioner'.

(R. Bunn collection)

SAXONE SHOE CO., RAMPANT HORSE STREET, c. 1930

This shop stood on the corner of Rampant Horse and Red Lion Streets. The Saxone Shoe shop is the same premises as those shown as H. P. Colman's in Volume 2, on page 19. The building, along with many well-known shops, including Curl's and Woolworth's, was destroyed during the blitz of 1942. Notice the hundreds of shoes on display and the advertisement — 16/9 (85p) for a pair of shoes!

(A. Williamson collection)

RAMPANT HORSE STREET, c. 1910

All this site on the south side of the street is now part of Marks & Spencer's store. The shops in this view include: at numbers 23 and 25, Snelling & Sons, confectioners and caterers; number 21, Horace Cockerill, milliner and fancy goods, above which was Goose's printing and bookbinding business; then A. H. Johnson & Co., hardware factors and, on the far right, the Spot Cash Tailor's shop.
(B. Gowen collection)

LAMB INN YARD, ORFORD PLACE, c. 1905

This early motor-car is parked in the courtyard of the Lamb Inn, Orford Place. The inn, owned at the time by Youngs, Crawshay & Youngs Ltd., is still there today. (See Volume 1, page 44).

ORFORD PLACE, c. 1910

The two trams are standing in Orford Place with the tram shelter in the centre. The left-hand tram is a number 13, on the Unthank Road to Magdelan Road route. Curl's building, in the background, was destroyed in the blitz in 1942. This view is beyond recognition today.
(B. Gowen collection)

CASTLE HOTEL, c. 1950s

This view has changed considerably in recent years. The Castle Hotel and some of the adjoining shops have been demolished to make way for the Castle Mall development. The car in front of the Blind Institution shop is a Vauxhall Cresta and the one on the right is a Ford Zodiac. At the time of writing, a new building is under construction on this site which, at the rear, will form the White Lion Street entrance to the Castle Mall. For a view of the opposite side of the street see Volume 3, page 39.

(R. Bunn collection)

CASTLE AND DAVEY PLACE, NORWICH

DAVEY PLACE, c. 1908

Davey Place — probably Norwich's first pedestrian way — was built in 1813, by Alderman Jonathan Davey. On the left, the businesses include:— Tyler's boot and shoe shop (notice the unusual lights over the windows); a restaurant; Stead & Simpson's shoe shop and, in the left background, Tyce's ironmongery. The Castle is in the background, behind Davey Steps. On the right, the businesses include:— The Jenny Lind public house; Brenner's Bazaar (the white building) and, in the right background, Fletcher's printing works.

(M. Dixon collection)

BRANDING HORSES, August, 1914

These two horses had been purchased by the army and are being branded in a side street adjacent to the Cattle Market and looking towards Cattle Market Street. On the left is A. Pank & Son, engineers, now Keller's tool shop, and, on the right is the Shirehall public house which was very popular with farmers and dealers on market days. The photograph was taken during the first month of World War 1.

(A. Williamson collection)

N 14   NORWICH. CATTLE MARKET

NORWICH CATTLE MARKET, c. 1950s

A later view than some of the illustrations shown in this series. The motorised cattle floats, parked under the trees, include those owned by R. W. Tufts of Attleborough and Mr Leggett. This area is now part of the Castle Mall development. Will the proposed concrete sheep ever be as attractive as this view?!

NORWICH FROM THE AIR, c. 1910

The Castle is seen in the centre of the picture with the Castle Gardens in the foreground. Five Norwich churches, St Andrew's Hall and several factory chimneys can be seen in the background. The area surrounding the Castle is now the Castle Mall Shopping Precinct development.

NORFOLK COUNTY CLUB, c. 1910

This fine Georgian building, at 17 Upper King Street, was built in the eighteenth century and became the premises of Harvey & Hudson's Bank until 1886. The Norfolk County Club purchased the building in 1887, at a cost of £3,600. Previously the Club had used rented accommodation on Guildhall Hill. After various alterations, the Club moved into the building in December, 1888. Today, the building remains the same externally but without the creeper and lamp standard.

(A. Williamson collection)

NORFOLK DAIRY FARMERS ASSOCIATION, PRINCE OF WALES ROAD, c. 1905

The Norfolk Dairy Farmers Association shop with its superb frontage was situated at 60-62, Prince of Wales Road. Notice particularly the dairy farm scenes on the tiles below the windows and the elaborate surrounds. The window displays are very appealing with a selection of meats, sausages, jars and packets along with a few pot plants. All that remains today are the decorative numbers '60' and '62', the shop front having been modernised with the doorway moved to the right. The site is now occupied by the Belmonte Restaurant.

(R. Bunn collection)

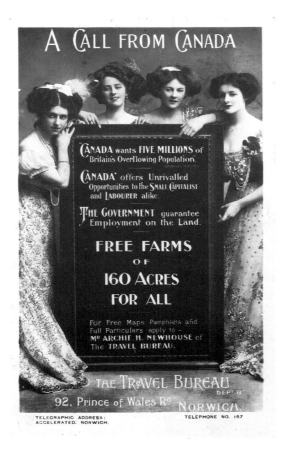

"A CALL FROM CANADA", c. 1913

A delightful advertising postcard that was published by the Travel Bureau, 92 Prince of Wales Road. "Canada wants FIVE MILLION of Britain's overflowing population . . . . Free farms of 160 acres for all". It was a very tempting offer and many Norwich and Norfolk people emigrated to Canada at this time. (See also Volume 1, page 50).
(R. Bunn collection)

JAMES STUART GARDEN, ST. FAITH'S LANE, 1922

This garden was a gift to the city of Norwich from Laura Elizabeth Stuart, in memory of her husband, James Stuart, Privy Councillor, of Carrow Abbey. The gateway was completed in 1922, its construction having been delayed by the First World War. This postcard shows the official opening of the garden with the Lord Mayor, Mrs. Stuart, civic dignitaries and the bearers of the city's regalia in attendance.

(A. Williamson collection)

PRINCE OF WALES ROAD, p.u. 1942

A number 90 'bus, on its way to Thunder Lane, passes an R.A.C. patrolman beside his motor-cycle and sidecar parked on the right, outside the Norwich Motor Company Garage. On the left, the shops include a cobbler, confectioner and, further along, Lambert's, tobacconist, with Delves Garage beyond.

(E. J. Read collection)

MARCANTONIO'S,
ROSE LANE, c. 1920s

Marcantonio's fish shop stood on the corner of Rose Lane and Eastbourne Place. Mr Marcantonio is seen in the right-hand side of the doorway, with Mrs Mildred Secker in the background and Mrs Nellie Capocci in front. Today, the site is occupied by Domino's Pizza.

THE JEWISH SYNAGOGUE

The Jewish Synagogue stood in Synagogue Street on the corner with Mountergate Street. It was destroyed in the blitz on 27th June, 1942. A picture of the gutted building can be seen in *Norwich at War* by Joan Banger.

O. Farrow, Proprietor — Norwich

ST. FAITH'S TAVERN, c. 1912

The proprietor, Mr Oscar Farrow, stands in the doorway of St. Faith's Tavern, at 17 Mountergate Street, at the junction of Synagogue Street. This was one of many corner public houses in Norwich, and was owned by Morgans, the local brewery. Notice the cellar flap to the left of the front door.

THE JOLLY MALTSTERS

This public house, owned by the Courage Brewery, stood on the corner of Carrow Road and King Street. At the time of this photograph it was "for sale" and was eventually demolished in the 1980s to allow for road widening and to improve visibility at this busy junction. On the opposite corner is the Kingsway public house, fomerly the Cellar House.
(B. Gowen collection)

CARROW SCHOOL ANNUAL OUTING, 1912

In 1912, the Carrow School outing was on board the pleasure steamer *Jenny Lind,* here seen passing Colman's Works.
Volume 3, page 96, gives more details about the school which catered for 277 boys and 225 girls. Well over 100 girls can
be seen on the top deck of the *Jenny Lind.*
(R. Bunn collection)

EVERARD VESSELS LOADING AND DISCHARGING AT NORWICH, NORFOLK

RIVERSIDE

This artist's impression of Everard's vessels loading and discharging their cargos was published as an advertising card for F. T. Everard & Sons Ltd., of Colchester and London. R. J. Read's flour mill can be seen on the left. Such a view will never be seen again since the construction of the new southern bypass has prevented coasters of this size reaching this section of the river.

Riverside, Norwich

5663

GREAT EASTERN HOTEL, RIVERSIDE, c. 1910

The Great Eastern Hotel has now been demolished and is the site of the Hotel Nelson. To the right of the Great Eastern Hotel one can just see the then Norfolk Railway Tavern public house. The notice above Foundry Bridge reads: "Norwich Motor Co. Ltd. welcomes you to the City". Behind the sign is the roof of James Porter, timber merchants. The numbers on the boats tied up at the Hotel are: Y273 and Y366.

BISHOP BRIDGE ROAD, 1910

The message on the reverse of this postcard states: "16th (Queens) Lancers, 23rd April, 1910". Here, the parade is seen passing down Bishop Bridge Road, no doubt coming from the Cavalry Barracks. Notice the tram tracks in the centre of the road. The sign on the right-hand house is Weeds Square, where flats have now been built.

ENGINE SHEDS, NORWICH THORPE STATION

Photographed looking towards the city from Carrow Road. Details of the locomotives, from left to right, are: tank engine — unknown; centre — B12 express locomotive 4-6-0, no 8569; right back — tank engine — unknown; right centre — B12 express locomotive 4-6-0, no 8523; right front — J17 goods locomotive 0-6-0, no 8213. The B12s were developed from the famous "Claud Hamilton" 4-4-0s.

(B. Gowen collection)

THORPE ROAD, ROSARY ROAD JUNCTION, c. 1908

On the left of this view, Stracey Road joins Thorpe Road and a tram is seen approaching the loop at the junction with Rosary Road. Notice the letter box and the sign on the tram standard which states: "You may telephone from here", referring to the post office on the corner. This was also a chemist's shop, run by Mr A. Colin Brown.
(B. Gowen collection)

SCOTT MEMORIAL CHURCH, THORPE ROAD

The Scott Memorial Church was designed in 1901 by A. H. Scott and erected as a memorial to his father, Jonathan Scott, a former Methodist minister. It closed in August, 1985, and has now been converted into offices. Once again, the building looks the same today but the railings have been removed. It is now called the Scott Memorial Hall.

Bridewell Alley,
Norwich

BRIDEWELL ALLEY, c. 1920

At the time of this photograph, the business second from the left was owned by a Mr Claxton, chiropodist and medical botanist. Hovell's, on the right, was listed as a toy dealer, but baskets can be seen on display. St. Andrew's Church stands in the background. Bridewell Alley looks much the same today. For details of the Bridewell Museum, see Volume 2, page 41.

TECHNICAL SCHOOL, c. 1911

This view is taken from Blackfriars Bridge looking up St. George's Street to St. Andrew's Hall, in the background. Norwich Technical Institute was erected in 1899, from designs by Mr Arthur E. Collins, city architect, and Mr W. Douglas Wiles, at a cost of £22,000. It was constructed in red brick with a stone portico. The School of Art was on the top floor. In 1912, both these schools were attended by 810 students. The building remains today as the Norwich Institute of Art and Design, which also occupies a large building opposite the Institute.

Old Model School.

THE MODEL SCHOOL, ST. ANDREW'S

This shows the entrance to the Girl's Model School at St. Andrew's which moved to Dereham Road in 1930. The school building itself was added and incorporated with an Elizabethan mansion, which was believed to have been occupied by Francis Rugge, Member of Parliament for the city and three times its mayor between 1587 and 1602. For some years after the school closed, the building was used as St. Andrew's Parish Hall. All that remains today is the arched doorway, which is the entrance to the Norwich Area Telephone Museum.

(A. Williamson collection)

CHARING CROSS, c. 1908

The photographer who took this postcard picture was looking towards St. Benedict's Street, on the left, with a number 27 tram, its destination shown as Aylsham Road. Behind the tram is The Vine public house. On the right of St. Benedict's Street — No 1 — is the city office of the Mapperley Colliery Co. Ltd., whose depot was situated at City Station. Westwick Street leads away to the right, behind the lady walking in the centre of the road — an impossibility with the volume of traffic today.

(B. Gowen collection)

ST. LAWRENCE CHURCH, NORWICH.

ST. LAWRENCE CHURCH

The Church of St. Lawrence is situated between St. Benedict's and Westwick Street, and built in the Perpendicular style throughout with a hammer-beam roof running the full length of the church. The square west tower is 112ft. high, having a staircase turret with spirelet on the north-west angle, a clock and six bells . This view is taken from St. Benedict's with St. Lawrence Little Steps on the left, and St. Lawrence Steps are on the right with Bullards Brewery in the background; this part of the brewery still remains as offices. St. Lawrence's is now under the care of the Norwich Historic Churches Trust, who are organising funds for restoration.

58

GIBSON'S PUMP,
WESTWICK STREET

The pump was erected in the boundary wall of Bullard's Brewery, in 1576, when the brewery was built by Robert Gibson and he had to bring water to the street. When the property was converted into flats, the pump was dismantled and re-erected on the other side of the wall and now faces the Anchor Quay development. An inscription reads: "Water here came from St. Lawrence's Well".

(A. Williamson collection)

ENTRANCE TO CORPORATION YARD, WESTWICK STREET, c. 1905

On the extreme left, there is a tram standard and a gas lamp on the pavement. Next, the building with the gable was known as the 'monkey house' and had the inscription "Removed from Whitlingham and rebuilt A.D.1900". This was another building that was burned down during the air raids of April, 1942. On the right are the gates to the corporation yard where there is a steam wagon in the background.

(B. Gowen collection)

GEORGE GREEN, ST. BENEDICT'S STREET, c. 1905

George Green, tailor, hatter and outfitter, was situated at nos. 42-44 St. Benedict's Street. The window displays are impressive and the signs above read, from left to right: 'Mechanic's & butchery clothing of all kinds'; 'Hardwearing school suits'; 'Smart waterproof overcoats'; 'Latest novelties in suits and neckwear' and, lastly, 'This is Green's'.
(R. Bunn collection)

W. MACE, ST. BENEDICT'S STREET, c. 1906

This wonderful advertising postcard shows the premises of W. Mace, boot and shoe merchant, fancy draper, millinery and dresses, situated at nos. 52, 54 and 56 St. Benedict's Street. A vast range of goods is displayed in the windows — with little room to spare. According to the 1912 directory, the shop also served as a post and money order office. Today, the property has been divided into three shops; no 52 is occupied by Age Concern. The large window, on the right of this picture, is still there along with the decorative top fascia board. Little Plough Yard is on the right.

A. PEROWNE & SON, ST. BENEDICT'S STREET, c. 1930

The well-known Norwich butcher, Mr A. Perowne, was situated at 81-83 St. Benedict's Street. Cooked meats and tinned goods are displayed in the left-hand window whilst, on the right, there are dozens of birds and an advertisement for best English tripe at 10d. per lb. The quality and quantity of poultry on display indicates that this picture was probably taken just before Christmas.

(R. Bunn collection)

BORROW HOUSE
NORWICH

GEORGE BORROW HOUSE
WILLOW LANE, c. 1930

George Borrow (1803-1881) author of *The Bible in Spain, Lavengro, Romany Rye* and *Wild Wales,* was born in Dumpling Green, East Dereham, and educated at Norwich Grammar School. He lived in this house from 1816 to 1824. The house was purchased and presented to the City of Norwich by Arthur Michael Samuel (later Lord Mancroft), during his lord mayoralty of 1912-13. Part of the house was a museum at the time. Although in a derelict condition today it looks much the same — even the shutters remain. The property is currently up for sale by the city authorities and its future is uncertain.

Y.M.C.A., POTTERGATE

The Y.M.C.A. Hostel — which previously had the title of Christian Alliance for Women and Girls Home — is seen here at 17 Pottergate. To its right, at no. 15, is Self Brothers, gas fitters. The old Y.M.C.A. building is now occupied by Marco's Restaurant. The other buildings remain the same with the exception of various shop front alterations, and the property on the far right — with the scaffolding — is now Lobo's Restaurant.

(A. Williamson collection)

8927 PRINCES ST OLD NORWICH—JUDGES L?º

PRINCES STREET, c. 1934

Princes Street runs from St. Andrew's Plain to Tombland. The Plumbers Arms Alley is on the left, beyond the first house and, further along is Tombland Alley (see Volume 2, page 33). The square, west tower of St. George's Church, Tombland, can be seen above the rooftops. On the right, but out of the picture, is Princes Street Congregational Chapel (see next page). Today, this quiet street remains unspoilt, having been tastefully restored and the premises being occupied by various offices and shops.

PRINCES STREET CONGREGATIONAL CHAPEL, c 1905

Built in 1819, the Chapel was extensively enlarged in 1869, under the Norwich architect, Edward Boardman. Standing on the south side of Princes Street, the building is the same today except for the railings which have been removed. It is now a United Reform Church. The Lecture Hall to the right of the Chapel, on the corner of Redwell Street, was built in 1879-80. It has just been refurbished internally, converted into offices and renamed Boardman House. The building on the left was P. Haldinstein's shoe factory, which ran through to Queen Street at that time.

ELM HILL

Two views of the same house and shop at 41-43 Elm Hill. W. H. West, scale maker, the name above the shop door, was mentioned in Kelly's directory for 1896. The timber-fronted facade (right) is the later version, very similar today and is now occupied by Henry Peek, wine merchant. The house was originally occupied by the Pettus family, including Thomas Pettus, Sheriff of Norwich in 1566 and Mayor in 1590.

Quay Side, from Fye Bridge.

QUAYSIDE, c. 1925

The buildings on the left have all been demolished. On the far right of Quayside is Beckwith Court (see Volume 2, page 36). The tall building was once a school, and then the Norwich Antique Centre which closed in May 1992. Next door was the new Star Inn, a Steward & Patteson public house, which was demolished in 1963; a three-storey unoccupied building now stands on this site.

TWO BREWERS,
MAGDALEN STREET, c. 1930s

Mr Benjamin Blogg, the proprietor, is standing in the doorway of the Two Brewers at 151 Magdalen Street, another public house owned by Morgan's Brewery. The notice in the right-hand window reads: 'Comfortable Lounge up the passage' — i.e. Two Brewers Yard, the entrance to which is just visible on the right and which is still there. At the time of writing, the building is empty and in a semi-derelict state, with the Two Brewers sign on the wall painted over.

DE CARLE'S DRUG STORES, ST. AUGUSTINE'S STREET, c. 1912

This shop at 9 St. Augustine's — just to the left of Rose Yard (see Volume 2, page 58) — was established in 1881, and owned by the De Carle family until 1929. The family produced patent medicines and fruit drinks. During the early years of the twentieth century, the property next door was used by De Carles for the manufacture of their products. The shop is now occupied by P. M. Coleman, optician.

(A. Williamson collection)

GILDENCROFT MEETING HOUSE. NORWICH.

GILDENCROFT MEETING HOUSE, c. 1912

The Gildencroft Meeting House is situated at the end of Gildencroft and can be reached from Chatham Street or via the footpath beside St. Augustine's Church. The Society of Friends opened the Meeting House in 1699. The building was gutted in the blitz of April, 1942; it was replaced, in 1958, by a smaller, single-storey building, which incorporated parts of the original house. At present, it is used by the Treehouse Children's Centre. The burial ground beside the Meeting House is still kept in a clean and tidy condition

NICHOLS BROS., ST. AUGUSTINE'S STREET, c.1908

Nichols Bros., pastry cooks and confectioners, was situated at 12 St. Augustine's on the corner of Sussex Street. Notice the two delivery handcarts on the left and, also, the advertisements for Vienna and wholemeal bread, and Hovis bread "as supplied to H.M. the King". The premises are occupied by Norwich Windsurfing today.
(R. Bunn collection)

ANGEL ROAD BRANCH.

NORWICH CO-OPERATIVE SOCIETY LTD.

This branch of the Norwich Co-operative Society stood at the junction of Angel and Patteson Roads (see Volume 3, page 95). The shop's handcart is on the left and three of the staff are standing in the doorway in their immaculate white coats and long aprons. Today, the premises have been slightly altered and are used by Bex Wholesale Warehouse Ltd.
(R. Bunn collection)

ST. MARTIN'S ROAD, c. 1910

St. Martin's Road is a continuation of Oak Street to its junction with Drayton and Aylsham Roads. The houses with the open turrets where destroyed in the blitz of 1942 but have been replaced by modern houses. The row of houses on the right , from the junction of St. Mary's Road, are still standing.

(A. Williamson collection)

THE GREAT FIRE, AYLSHAM ROAD, June, 1908

This is the scene after the fire at the premises of Mr Herbert Goff, tallow maker, and Mr Remblant, hoop and hurdle maker, on Aylsham Road next to the Windmill Public House. This postcard was posted on 24th June, just two days after the fire and shows Mr Remblant, second right.

(R. Bunn collection)

TOLL HOUSE, AYLSHAM ROAD. NORWICH.

AYLSHAM ROAD, c. 1910

Aylsham Road at the Boundary Road junction — an unrecognizable scene compared with the same view today! The old toll house stands on the left and, under the trees, is the Boundary Cross. One of ten around the city, it was moved in the 1930s for safety reasons but, unfortunately, was demolished by a lorry and never restored.
(A. Williamson collection)

SNOWFLAKE LAUNDRY, c. 1904

This very rare postcard is included because it shows a typical horse-drawn delivery vehicle as was seen in the streets of Norwich during the early part of the century. The cart was owned by the Snowflake Laundry of 169 Bull Close Road, Norwich.

(B. Gowen collection)

MAGDALEN ROAD, c. 1911

Looking from Magdalen Gates along Magdalen Road, this is a similar view to that shown in Volume 1, page 90. However, this one shows a procession of three decorated trams, led by no. 19, while a large crowd looks on. The occasion is unknown.

(A. Williamson collection)

'THE HERO', GEORGE BRODIE

George Brodie was one of two people who lost their lives in the disastrous floods of August, 1912. After saving many adults and children, it is believed that he lost his footing and drowned in the strong current. The other person to die was a baby who fell into the water while being rescued with her mother. A woman also died from shock and fright whilst being rescued.

NORWICH FLOODS (1), DERBY STREET, 27th August, 1912

This and the following four views are of streets affected by the floods and are all in the area of the River Wensum. These are also views of streets not normally seen on postcards. The depth of the water in Derby Street can be gauged by the hubs of the wheels on the cart. At this time, Derby Street ran from Midland Street to Heigham Street.

(M. Dixon collection)

CREAT FLOOD AT NORWICH. AUGUST 27 28 1912.   OAK STREET.

NORWICH FLOODS (2), OAK STREET, August, 1912

On the left, the row of houses and shops have been tastefully restored in recent years. In the left foreground is Talbot Yard, next is Edmund Barker's barber shop and then Dog Yard — just two of the many yards in Oak Street. The area after the three-storey block is now taken up by St. Crispin's dual carriageway. On the far right is the White Lion public house, now the Tap and Spile. Near the junction of Station Road — leading to City Station — is St. Martin's at Oak Mission Hall. Then comes the shop and sub post office of Mr Harry Rudd, which is still a newsagent's today. A plaque on the wall of the shop reads: "Anguish Boys Charity 1901". At the time of writing the second shop is derelict and the near one has disappeared. Notice the tram wires from Station Road to Sussex Street — these were out of use during the floods.

NORWICH FLOODS (3), LOTHIAN STREET, September, 1912

The only transport in Lothian Street — which ran from Barn Road to Orchard Street — was by rowing boat, as seen in this photograph. P.C.103.is looking at the camera. During 26th and 27th August, 7.34 inchs of rain were recorded. The flood sluices at New Mills were opened and, eventually, the water reached 6 feet above normal summer level.

NORWICH FLOODS (4), ORCHARD STREET, August, 1912

This view of Orchard Street is looking towards the junction with Midland Street which joined it at that time. On the left-hand side, at the corner of Exeter Street, is Bassingthwaighte's Stores. Opposite, on the right but behind the well-loaded cart, is Cardigan Street. Notice the people watching from their bedroom windows
(M. Dixon collection)

NORWICH FLOODS (5), MAGDALEN STREET, August, 1912

In Magdalen Street, no trams could run and only horse-drawn transport could operate. Looking towards the city, the horses and carts are seen passing no. 40, Alderson's, bootmaker, and no. 42, the King's Head public house; the publican at this time was Mr Charles Nixon. The King's Head is the same today, as are the upper storeys of the other buildings, with various shops beneath. Christie's, auctioneers, now occupy the building on the right.

HARRY DANIELS, V.C.

Harry Daniels was born at Wymondham on 13th December, 1884, the son of William Daniels, baker and confectioner. He lost both his parents when he was four-years-old and was brought up in the Boys' Home in St. Faith's Lane, Norwich. He joined the army in 1903, and served for many years in India, eventually being promoted to Company Sergeant-Major in December, 1914. He was awarded the Victoria Cross (London Gazette, 28th April, 1915): "Harry Daniels, No. 9665, Company Sergt.-Major, 2nd. Battn. Rifle Brigade, (The Prince Consort's Own). For most conspicuous gallantry on 12th March, 1915, at Neuve Chappelle, France. When their battalion was impeded in the advance to the attack by the wire entanglements and subjected to very severe machine-gun and rifle fire, along with Corporal Noble, voluntarily rushed in front and succeeded in cutting the wire. Both men were wounded, Cpl. Noble later dying of his wounds". Harry Daniels was commissioned in July, 1915, awarded the Military Cross in March, 1916, and, after a distinguished career, rose to the rank of Lieutenant Colonel.

This photograph was taken in the grounds of the Boys' Home after a civic reception in the Guildhall, in 1915. His wife is on his right, surrounded by guardians of the Home. Harry Daniels died in Leeds, on 13th December, 1953.
(R. Bunn collection)

NORWICH FLORAL FESTIVAL, May, 1908

A very unusual photograph of the Norwich Floral Festival. Each girl appears to be holding up a fish and has more in her basket. What is the connection with a floral festival?

(R. Bunn collection)

MAGDALEN GATE.
(OUTSIDE)

J.KIRKPATRICK.1720.   H.NINHAM.1864.

POCKTHORPE GATE.
(OUTSIDE)

J.KIRKPATRICK.1720.   H.NINHAM.1864.

THE CITY GATES

These are views of the Pockthorpe Gate at Barrack Street and Magdalen Gate at Magdalen Street, from the set of postcards on Norwich Gates, published by Jarrold's (see also Volume 2, page 13 and Volume 3, page 9).

89

THE RED LION, EATON, c.1905

The background to this picture has completely changed with houses on the left, traffic lights on the junction of Bluebell Road and Church Lane and the removal of the telegraph poles which lined the A11 for many years. Nobody would walk down the middle of this road today! The Red Lion, owned by the Norwich brewers Steward and Patteson, is little changed today.

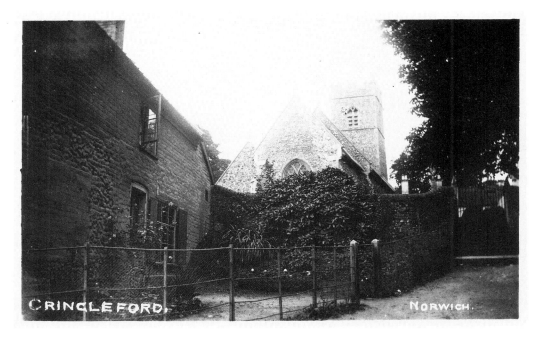

CRINGLEFORD, c. 1910

This view of Cringleford shows St. Peter's Church, built of flint in the Perpendicular style, close to the old route of the A11. The cottage on the right has been demolished.

THE STREET, TROWSE, c. 1920
A group of military horsemen are seen passing through Trowse, with St. Andrew's Church in the background.

CHURCH of ST ANDREW ~ WHITLINGHAM, NORWICH. (Ruins)

WHITLINGHAM CHURCH

The Church of St. Andrew was desecrated in about 1630 but, standing beside the River Wensum, it forms a picturesque ruin with its round Norman tower.

Thorpe Village, Norwich

THORPE VILLAGE, c. 1908

Leaving the city on the A47, the twin gables on the left can still be seen today. In the background is the spire of Thorpe Church (see Volume 2, page 101). The cottage on the right remains and Thorpe Old Hall is behind the wall. This road became known as 'Thorpe narrows' and was widened to alleviate traffic congestion. Today's flow of heavy traffic has been eased by the opening of the southern bypass in September, 1992.

SCENE OF THE CATTON MURDER. Spixworth Road.
Where the body was found X. NR NORWICH. OCT 29th 1908.

SCENE OF THE CATTON MURDER, 1908

This postcard shows a group of people standing at the spot where the body was found. The message on the back reads: "Just a p.c. Hoping this will find Aunt better. I thought I would send this p.c. to add to your collection. The murdered woman was nineteen-year-old Eleanor Howard of Hainford, and her sweetheart, Horace Larter of Norwich, gave himself up soon after the body was dicovered. The murder was committed with a 1/- clasp knife bought a few days before at Pearson's the cutlers" (see also Volume 2, page 56).

ST. FAITH'S UNION

St. Faith's Union was a red-brick building erected as a house of industry in 1805. It served Coltishall and thirteen other parishes. It was enlarged in 1849, and again in 1862, to accommodate 500 persons. The site is now occupied by St. Faith's Crematorium.

THE SCHOOL, COSTESSEY, c. 1912

This school building still stands on the corner of Longwater Lane; it is now called St. Augustine's Roman Catholic Primary School. It was erected in 1871, for 200 children, and enlarged in 1904, under the patronage of Lord Stafford, D.S.O. The Sisters of Charity of St. Paul were the teaching staff. The building remains much the same today, in spite of some minor alterations.
(R. Bunn collection)

NORWICH MOTOR-CYCLE CLUB, RINGLAND
The hill climb trials at Ringland. Note the local registration number — CL 1377 — on the upright machine; the other motor-cycle appears to have had a slight accident.
(M. Dixon collection)

MOTOR-CAR TRIALS AT RINGLAND, 1930

The Singer motor-car, registration CL 1639, is seen at Ringland Hills. Motor-car trials took place at the same time as the motor-cycle trials. Some of the motor-cycles can be seen lying on the grass in the right background (see also Volume 3, page 91).
(M. Dixon collection)

NORWICH UNION LIFE INSURANCE SOCIETY

An advertising postcard, overprinted as a New Year card, shows the marble hall at the Head Office of the Norwich Union, Surrey Street. Refurbishment has taken place, and Norwich Union is one of the city's largest employers , with offices in various buildings around the city.

(M. Dixon collection)

BACKS LTD. 1908

Backs Ltd. had premises in Norwich, Great Yarmouth and Lowestoft — hence the nautical comic scene. Published for use as a representative's calling card, it stated on the reverse that the representative would call on a customer on Wednesday, 6th June, 1908.

(R. Bunn collection)

JAS. CHAMBERLIN & SMITH,
Pheasant & Poultry Food Merchants,
(THE FIRST MANUFACTURERS),

POST OFFICE STREET, NORWICH,

ESTABLISHED FORTY YEARS.

SOLE PROPRIETORS OF THE
CELEBRATED AROMATIC SPANISH MEAL, D. S. MEAT GREAVES, KALŸDÉ
CANADIAN POULTRY MEAL, CAYCAR EXCELSIOR, ETC.

Only Award for Game Food, Paris Exhibition, 1878.
Bronze Medal & Diploma, Manheim, 1880. Silver Medal, Cléves, 1881.
Gold Medal & Diploma of the Société Belge D'Avicultura, 1884.
Silver Medal, International Exhibition, Antwerp, 1885.
Honourable Mention, Paris Exhibition, 1889.
PURVEYORS BY SPECIAL WARRANT TO H.R.H. THE PRINCE OF WALES.

JAS. CHAMBERLIN & SMITH

This is an advertising postcard for Jas. Chamberlin & Smith, pheasant and poultry food merchants, of Post Office Street, Norwich. Notice the list of special awards gained at exhibitions during the 1870s and 1880s, and the special warrant to H.R.H. The Prince of Wales. The lower half of Exchange Street was known as "Post Office Street" until the 1870s. In Kelly's directory for 1912, Chamberlin's was situated at 27 Exchange Street.

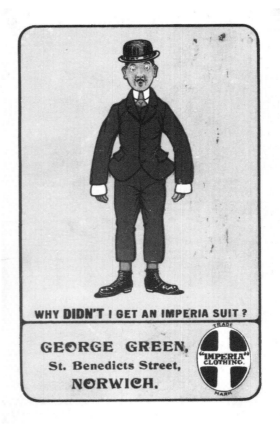

COMIC ADVERTISING

On the left, a card with a motoring theme for Mann Egerton & Co. Ltd. of 5 Prince of Wales Road, was drawn by G. E. Shepheard, a well-known postcard illustrator. The card was posted in 1909. On the right, an amusing card for George Green, outfitters, shows the importance of buying a well-fitting suit by Imperia Clothing! For a view of Green's shop see page 61.

(Mann Egerton card from B. Gowen collection; George Green card from R. Bunn collection)

"COME TO NORWICH", c. 1912

Known as a 'pull-out' postcard, a flap opens to reveal a concertina strip of views of Norwich. Published by Valentine's, this type of stock card would be issued for various cities and towns, and overprinted to order. The appropriate strip of pictures would then be fixed under the flap.

"WHY WE SING ABOUT NORWICH", c. 1914

Another Valentine's 'pull-out' card with its strip of photographs — "look under my wing, and no longer you'll doubt that Norwich has a lot to sing about". Norwich was a large canary breeding area and Norwich City Football Club are nicknamed the 'Canaries'. See also *Norwich City: A Portrait in Old Picture Postcards* — also published in this series

WHY WE SING ABOUT NORWICH

Look under my wing, and no longer you'll doubt
That Norwich has a lot to sing about.

ACKNOWLEDGEMENTS

The author is very grateful to the following people without whom this book would not have been possible:—

For the loan of postcards:—
Rhoda Bunn, Michael Dixon, Basil Gowen, Eric Read and Tony Williamson.

Edited by Steve Benz
Additional editing by Gillian Jackson.